SUCCESS AT YOUR DOOR STEPS

YOUR GUIDE TO A FASTER CLIMB AT THE HIERARCHICAL LADDER OF SUCCESS

M.G.W. AGUILAR

ISBN: 9798648519930

Foreword

Who said that professional success should cost you half of your life? Who said that you have to experience failure before you reach the top? Who said that you have to be at least 40 to become manager of a multi-billion company? Who said that you need to have at least 5 years of service in the company to get that promotion you ever wanted? Success comes in several ways; most often takes time and a lot of hard work, but sometimes does not come at all. This book will make you realize that success is not really a journey as long as what most people say. This will open your eyes to the shortcuts life has to offer in reaching your goals. Have you been working all your life, but still got nothing? It is not yet too late for you; you still have a chance to achieve what you have been dreaming of. Are you someone who is just starting taking the first steps of the ladder of success? Don't waste your time and efforts believing in what many had believed in but has led them to failure. Together, let us celebrate the faster way to success. Written by a visionary and an expert in leadership, this book is expected to change lives and be criticized by many.

CONTENTS

Chapter 1: Defining your Goal   1

- Getting ready for your Goal   3
- What is Success to you?   7
- Writing down your Goal   14

Chapter 2: The Goal and the way to it   17

- Is the Goal more important
  than the Journey?   19
- Finding the right way   21
- There is no impossible Goal   25
- The Shortcut to your Goal   29

Chapter 3: Getting to your Goal   41

- The risk of believing in the wrong path   43
- Seven Ingredients that will pave
  your way to success   45

**Chapter 4:
Telling your success story & inspiring others**   55

- Sharing your story   57
- Inspire others and teach them how to fish   59

Bonus Chapters   63

CHAPTER 1

DEFINING YOUR GOAL

Success is only for those who start working today

Prof. Mark Gabriel Wagan Aguilar

Getting Ready for your Goal

In the study conducted by MidAmerica Nazarene University on 2018, only 25% of Americans was able achieve their dream job. Sad but true, most of us in spite of everything we have done over the years just to get that pay check, respect, and self-worth ended nowhere but in the same job. What can you do about it? There are people better than you, there are people who are more flexible, resilient, efficient, and liked than you, and what hurts more, you were already there before they even came. Is it game over? Is job promotion really not for you? Is life really sucking you? What should you do?

We all know that our parents tend to say that someone needs to go to school and perform excellently to secure a good future, unfortunately, if there is one thing I won't tell my children about, it is that. Though has a major contribution to job security, school may

secure you a job that would support your everyday living, but definitely does not guarantee you the success you want in life, at least for the most people I know. According to Anna Chui, a communication expert and a life enthusiast, not all who succeed in school, succeed in life. She pointed out the following why this happens:

- What you need for a good and successful life is not really learned at school
- Doing bad at school doesn't make you a failure
- Life is a really long lesson, so long that you can't define a person's success by just one section of it

You must be thinking of why you did you spend almost twenty years of your life attending classes and learning things that seems to be irrelevant in real life setting and in the professional work environment. Although, it is likely to be true that there are subjects being taught in school that are not related to the field you want to be at in the future, these courses are there to develop your ability to learn, modify your attitude, and hone your skills, nonetheless, we cannot deny that what may be good for your teachers might not be enough for the people you will be dealing with after graduating.

Did you attend the last reunion of your batch? Do you still see your childhood friends and classmates way back your school days? Like other people, do you also wonder how the least performing student in your class years ago has become the manager of the multi-billion-dollar company you have always dreamt of working with, and how your friend who was always tardy in class became one of the promising businessmen of the country? Several researches has determined that your shortcomings as a student do not make as a failure, you are not encouraged to drop out from school, but you should understand that there are other things that matters aside from having a high grade, and that is consistency. If you are good in school, you should be able to perform great in the professional work environment as well, but if you are having a difficult time in school, at least make sure to pass, and just push yourself to be excellent after.

Success is permanent and Failure isn't fatal
Mike Ditka

According to Mike Ditka, success will be there with you once you have achieved it, but don't be afraid to fail as it won't kill you. This may be true, but do not make it to the point that you have been failing unceasingly, you no longer know the meaning of success.

Lessons in life differ from one person to another; there is no one size fits all in education and in life experiences. Your teachers may teach you fundamentals and the technicalities of a field, but it is really life who teaches you lessons every day. It is simply never ending, and these lessons are what would make a better person. You however should not be reluctant to those lessons and to changes, as these may motivate you to see things differently.

What is success to you?

Success is difficult to define, especially if you have not experience it yet. According to dictionaries, success is something that one aims to achieve, a goal, an attainment, an accomplishment. Start asking yourself now, what is success to you? What do you aim in life? What do you want to attain? What do you want to accomplish? You and not what others want for you. Is it getting your dream job? Having a wonderful family? Calling a beach house your home? Or to take sit in the top management meeting of your company? No matter what success is to you, no one should stop you from reaching it! Write it down now, and instead of thinking about it as goal, see it as your purpose in life, that if you will not achieve it, you have failed a person. It may sound a little bit scary and challenging in a way, but your attitude towards your goal is important.

Based on research, people with goals are ten times more likely to succeed, however, in the study of Allaboutcareers.com among 38,500 estimated; a whopping 52% said that they don't know what they want after graduation. These students have already spent 4-5 years of their lives learning specific industries and types of work, but they still end up with no idea of what they want to be. What if after graduation, they realize that they would like to establish a career in a different industry, making his degree irrelevant? What is he going to with his degree? What about the 4-5 years he have spent? This is why you should know what success is to you as early as now. The time in setting your goal is limited, some will say that as long as you are breathing, you may still reach your dreams, it may be true, but you won't be able to maximize it and enjoy it to the fullest. Think now. The clock is ticking.

**A person should set his goals
as early as he can
and devote all his energy
and talent to getting there**
Walt Disney

If until now you are still unsure about what you really want in life, you should stop and breathe for a while; you might be wasting time for doing something that would not help you in reaching your goals. Success does not have to be represented by only one goal; success to you can be two, three, or more objectives in life. It depends on you; just make sure that you are serious about those.

Pointers on how to determine your goal:

- Determine what makes you happy
- Know where you are comfortable with
- Know your weaknesses and strengths
- Identify your resources
- Determine the opportunities and threats

Determine what makes you happy

It could be anything. Who and what makes you smile? A goal should give you satisfaction, so if you don't see a goal in mind to make you happy and satisfied, it is not the right goal for you.

Know where you are comfortable with

This does not necessarily mean that you will just focus on what you are good at. Knowing where you are comfortable with is about in what field do you think you can show who you really are, where you can introduce the real you without hiding from anybody or anything. By being comfortable, you would be able maximize your strengths and possibly overcome your weaknesses.

Know your weaknesses and strengths

Are you able to determine the days of the week when you are most excited to wake up and go to school? There is always that one to two subjects being taught in school where you like the most, because it is where you are most likely to get high grades. While there are these days when you are least motivated because of that subject you hate most. Evaluate what you do in those subjects where you perform best at with the other 4 tips; the right goal for you might be in this field.

Identify your resources

Do you have what it takes to do what you think you want to do in life? Do you the means? You can't get to your goal without having the means to it, that is why you have determine what are the things you need to do in order to achieve your goal, and what are the things that you need to have to do what you need to do in order to attain the goal. If you don't have these means, or if you are not capable of developing it over time, the goal you have in mind is not for you. You might just end up wasting years of your life trying to reach it, when it has been too obvious from the start that it is not the right goal for you.

Determine Opportunities and Threats

No man is an island. You may think that you don't need to consider other factors but yourself to reach your goal, but as much as we want to believe in that, it is untrue. There are several external factors that we have to consider when choosing our target in life. These are the opportunities and threats existing beyond our control. How can you achieve a goal if the opportunities that would walk you through challenges to attain your goal are not present within your reach? Overseas

Filipino Workers for example, chose to work in other countries because they were unable to find opportunities in the Philippines that would help them to reach their goal; the success that they set seem to be unachievable in their place of residence. You should also identify the threats that you are likely to face during the entire process, some are foreseeable, and some will just appear out of nowhere, you should be ready whatever happens. These threats are like typhoons and earthquakes, you should be ready by the time it comes, or else, you are hopeless. All of these are some reasons why some people fail to reach their dreams; it is either they are barking on the wrong dream or they are just simply not ready when obstacles got in their way.

> **Avoiding danger is no safer in the long run than outright exposure; the fearful are caught as often as the bold**
>
> **Helen Kellen**

Writing down your Goals

Goals we set in our minds might be impossible to some and sometimes also to you, but have you ever asked yourself what makes a goal impossible and possible? Is it the goal itself or are there other factors that have caused it? Keep in mind that not all "too good to be true" in this world is not true; if I asked you if it is possible to become a billionaire at a very young age without having wealthy parents before young entrepreneurs got featured in the news, you would have said no. To succeed in life, you have to understand that all goals are possible; you just need to know how you could achieve it. Based on research, writing down your goals increases your chances to getting to it. Michael Hyatt, the founder and CEO of Michael Hyatt and Company, has listed 5 reasons why you should commit your goals to writing:

- Because it will force you to clarify what you want
- Because it will motivate you to take action
- Because it will provide a filter for other opportunities
- Because it will help you overcome resistance
- Because it will enable you to see and celebrate your progress

Notice that you are more likely to memorize your lessons in school when you wrote them down? Attitude is important, and a motivation will definitely push you to pursuing something and working hard for it, motivation removes all the bad vibes and fuels your spirit. And that writing attached to you wall, at the desktop of your computer, at the front page your notebooks, will definitely remind you that you have a goal to pursue, which will act a motivation that pushes you to work through it.

This would also introduce you to things you want to do aside from what are written, as the more you see your written goal, the more you become hungry for it, or the more you become uninterested. It will act as an alarm clock, a reminder, something that no matter how you try to avoid it will be there as it is written. Put it on the wall, on your desktop, set it as wallpaper for your phone, as a sticky note on the mirror in your bedroom, and if you're studying at the cover or first page of your notebooks. What will make it more effective is if you write it down starting with "I AM" instead of "I WILL BE" or "TO BE". "I am the President of the United States of America"; instead of I will be the President of the United State of America. This won't allow you to resist, and would encourage you to just go with it, time will come; you will possess the personality a president has without you noticing.

CHAPTER 2

THE GOAL
& THE WAY TO IT

Change your ways, not your goals; don't give up and keep moving forward
Prof. Mark Gabriel Wagan Aguilar

Is the Goal more important than the Journey?

There are several ways. So does the way towards the goal matter more than the goal itself? The road matters more in a way that you should not just select randomly.

Some people might say that the first step to reach a goal is knowing where to go, however, critics say "how could you know the way to a goal without knowing the goal itself?" In an organizational behavior class with roughly ten students, the professor who is known to be a Human Resource Management Expert asked the students, which do they think is more correct between *"doing the right things"* and *"doing things right"* Among all the students, only one chose "doing things right". This may make you think that the answer of that one student is wrong, and the answer of the rest is more proper, but have you ever thought of why only a few are chosen to lead organizations? Why is there only one president of a country? And why is there only one head of the family? It is because the majority is not always right, thus, quality matters more than quantity. Going back to his answer, despite rejections received from his classmates and the professor, he carefully explained that one would not be able to know the right things to be done, without being guided by the right processes and policies, which being highlighted on the concept of "doing things right"; with the right procedures and policies, one would be able to do the right things, and not the other way around. The goal is defined by the steps to and it is not the procedures being defined by the goal. Going straight towards the goal without considering the right way to do it, will lead to the risk of making mistakes, which will result to trial and error. While choosing to know the better way on how to do things right, would avoid such complications.

A year after that classroom discussion, that student have published five researches in reputable international journals, got appointed as an editorial board member of a number of journals, and became a school director of an international business school.

There is no failure,
except in no longer trying
                    Elbert Hubbard

Finding the right way

Have you seen a movie with a scene where people have to choose between turning left and right towards their destination? Do you notice that most of the time, an obstructed road is the right way while the clear one is nothing but a trap? If only that is how easy it is, everyone probably has reached their goals in life already. In real life, it is not always like that. All alternative paths towards a goal is the right way to go, it just vary on difficulty, and distance. There is always a faster way without sacrificing the quality of work and experience, you just have to evaluate which path it is.

Let me share you a story. Once upon a time, two friends, Carlo and Jack where eating lunch together. They were fresh graduates from a community college and have been unemployed for 6 months already. The two were discussing about finding a job. Carlo was thinking about getting hired for an entry level position disregarding the salary, he was planning to stay in that company for a long period of time so he could get promoted and achieve success in the future. Jack however has a different perspective: he was thinking of getting a job that pays well, he was even considering demanding a rate, but was planning to only stay there for a maximum of one year, and then search for another employer where he will apply for a higher position and demand a better pay.

Most people would probably agree to the plan of Carlo as most of us grew up in a world where everyone thinks that you really have to start low, gain years and years of experiences, and then wait for the opportunity to knock. The entire process we have believed in usually takes decades and in most cases, a lifetime especially for people who have worked hard but ended up with nothing. However, in this story, that is not what happened. 3 years after, Jack became a restaurant manager while the Carlo is still in the same position, which he applied for 3 years ago.

There is always a way around it. Yes, you have read it right, there are shortcuts! Remember Super Mario Bros? It took me 16 years to save the princess; I have continuously failed for 16 years, until one day, out of nowhere, I have learned that there are shortcuts. Guided by a video I have watched through the internet, it took me only two hours to finish the game. It was crazy after learning that the game that I found impossible to finish is actually accomplishable within 2 hours. If only I have searched harder, I should have finished the game earlier and have not wasted time. It may not be Super Mario Bros. but I am sure that we can all relate to my experience.

Forget what your parents told you about waiting for the right opportunity and spending much time and effort to achieve something you want, and just stick to what your boss have been saying; "If you can finish it today, do it! Don't wait for tomorrow". So, if you can become manager today, go for it, don't just sit down in your office and wait for something or someone to open the door for you.

Remember, there is a shortcut for everything. Forget about others who say there are things with none; they just failed to find a faster way to become who they are now. Work harder, strive more, and don't waste time; you will end up more successful than those who started reaching out for their dreams before you did.

Time shall never be seen as an investment, hard work is.

> **Most people don't see that they have options beyond what society tells them to do. That's the biggest problem. They honestly believe that compliance is the shortcut to success**
>
> **Seth Godin**

There is no impossible Goal

Do you get easily demotivated? Are you the type of person who always thinks negatively? Are you the type of person who goes along with everybody's decision to stop? And are you someone who gives up easily? At least one 'yes" answer for any of these questions makes you unlikely to succeed in life. Yes, there may be shortcuts to success, but dreaming something faster than the fastest way possible will lead you to a more delayed journey. Make sure that the shortcut that you are taking is a real shortcut and not something that will pull you back from the start. Discipline is still important during your journey towards the goal, and yes, hard work is still needed.

A toilet that is very clean reflects how dedicated a janitor is to reach her goals in life, which makes him better than a supervisor who despite serving in a company for only a few months, poorly performs because of getting tired of waiting for his promotion, hence that makes the janitor more likely to achieve what he wants. What is being taught here is that a person needs to know when to stop and when not to, and understand that giving up easily is not necessary. What if the shortest shortcut to your dream will take you 100 steps, would you choose to stop at the 50th? You are very lucky if you know that it is a 100-step- journey, but in reality, it can't be determined until you reach the finish line. In the game called Super Mario Bros., there are two shortcuts going nearer to the final stage; the first one will lead you to world 4, and the second will lead to you to the final world. In between of these two shortcuts is only 1 area, obviously an easier way towards the goal of the game, but if you have found that area difficult to finish and give up in the middle of it, you would not know that the final stage is just a few steps away, thus, would demotivate you and lead you to letting your goal to finish the game slip away. And when are you going to try it again? After knowing that a friend have reached the second shortcut? Sadly, that won't happen in real life, as we have different goals, hence different journeys to take.

No one would know what is at the other corner of the bridge until someone has crossed the bridge.

You have probably seen this photo in social media more than once, and I bet you felt sorry for him. But have you looked at the mirror and ask if you should also need to feel sorry for yourself?

Whether you deny it or not, there have been times when are like this man. We all have been working so hard to reach our goals in life, but by the time we are already near to it, we suddenly stop and give up. Keep in mind that positivity keeps you going. No matter how difficult and impossible challenges may seem to be, there is always a way through it. Dedication is number one, hard work is second, and positivity is third. Never stop dreaming, and new stop working!

Take the challenge of your life. Reach out to your goals. There is no limit to what you can achieve
Lailah Gifty Akita

The Shortcut to your Goal

As I write this book, I search the internet for quotations, and I am surprised to see 99% of those posted in websites are stating that there is no shortcut to success, and what made me more surprise is learning that these statements came from known great men in various fields. My friends, they are wrong. Yes, I am invalidating what these people have said. It is not true that there is no shortcut. There is! As I have said, we have different goals in life, and the definition of success varies from one person to another. No one can really tell if what you are aiming does not have a shortcut.

What is really a shortcut? How do you define shortcuts? Is it a road that gives you clear sight to your goal? Is it a path shorter than the rest? Or is it an elevator where you just need to push a bottom and voila, there you are at the top. This is the problem! People literally think that the term shortcut refers to roads that will give them unobstructed and faster access going to their goal; that is what you call magic and not a shortcut. There is no physical road towards our dream and there is not even an elevator! So what is a shortcut?

The shortcut to your goal is only seen by yourself and is built with the following ingredients.

- Commitment
- Hard Work
- Focus
- Positivity
- Urgency
- Humility

- Competitive Attitude
- Rick-taking attitude
- Professionalism
- Self-Love

Commitment

Allow no one and nothing to stop reaching your goals. No matter how hard it may seem, have a winning attitude! Commitment is about having that determination and loyalty to your goal, thus, showing a do or die mindset.

Hard Work

Perhaps this is most difficult term to define. I have searched the internet several times trying to find a precise definition of hard work, however, all the definitions just lead me to more question. Generally, it is defined as "something that requires great effort"; however, come to think of it, when can an "effort" be considered great? To finally give a clear meaning for it, I have come with this "hard work is doing something beyond what other can do and what you think you can do". Working hard is an electrical fan trying to produce a level 4 wind power despite having a maximum power of 3. It is a basketball player who has missed a thousand free throw shots but still tried a 1001st. Push yourself to your limit, if it is not enough, go beyond, and I assure you, it is indeed worth it.

Now, how would you know if you are working hard enough? Benchmark! Look at others, and exceed what they have done. If your officemates have worked for 12 hours, work for 13 hours. If your classmate read a chapter of a book, read at least 2 chapters. Hard Work is about getting more, achieving more, and not settling for less. Hard Work pays off; it will lead to better results.

Focus

Focus is about having a good look at your goal and allowing no one or nothing distract you and remove your attention. Negligence can cost you years of hard work. It is important to focus on what you want, it is important to keep an eye on your prey; it can vanish within just a blink of an eye.

Positivity

Have you heard about the saying "thinking about something to happen, will allow it to happen"? Thinking about it will really help you to establish a deeper interest, a serious mindset, and a drive, which would lead to hard work. As mentioned, there is no impossible goal, but if you be will thinking that the goal you have been trying to achieve for a very long period of time is impossible, it is you who have turned it into an impossible goal, and not because of what really it is.

Personally, positive thinking has been my weapon to all the obstacles I have faced in life. And one think I have realized is that thinking positively can move mountains, dry seas, and can really change the direction of the wind.

Urgency

Don't take the baby steps! You are wasting your time! Most of us believes on the traditional way to success; sit down, do what is expected from you, and then wait for an opportunity to knock at the door. But what if nothing knocked? What if you have waited for a lifetime but still got nothing. Don't get blinded by such statements and stop wasting time, it does not work that way. Get on your feet and start running now; it is you who should look for the opportunities and not the other way around. Always remember that time is luxury.

Humility

Increase your self-esteem to increase your drive towards your goal. Stand up with pride, and shout out what you have accomplished today. Feeling proud of your achievements may be bragging to others, but it is not. Humility is not being pretentious, thus, if what you being proud of is true, then there is nothing wrong with it, in fact, it gives confidence that will be your ticket to greater heights.

Competitive Attitude

The professional work environment is a competition arena whether we admit it or not. It is full of people competing against each other for respect, power, recognition, and to see others fail. Surviving with the presence of people and circumstances that will try to pull you down is a part of life. Success is only for the strong and those who have the courage to pull others down so that they could push themselves up. Establish that competitive attitude and kick ass, unless you want stay forever at the bottom of the ladder.

Risk-Taking Attitude

What will make you stop from reaching your dreams? Risks? Then you are not worth it. You are better off achieving nothing in life.

Let me tell you a story. Three young people, Jason, Mark, and Patrick are standing at one end of a swamp and found out that there is a treasure at the other side of it. They have never seen this pond, thus, no one knows what are under its waters. They all know how to swim but are afraid of going across the waters as it looks scary; dark, quiet, covered by trees, and seems deep. Around the swamp is a 5 mile-walk because of series of trees blocking the way while across it is only about half of a kilometer. Jason though have been dreaming for several years of getting his family out from poverty refused to go for the treasure because of the hard ship he will go through if he chooses to go around the swamp and the risks of crossing the scary-looking swamp. He stepped back and left. Patrick on the other hand expressed his commitment in going for the treasure, like Jason he has been dreaming of getting her family out from poverty, and with his mindset on the "slowly but surely" process and because of the scare the swamp has gave him, he chose to go around the swamp. Meanwhile, Mark took a deep breath and thought of how important the treasure is for him. With Patrick on his way to the treasure, he chose to go across the swamp riding a log and bringing a huge branch of a tree to scare away wild animals. Mark ended up with the treasure. The swamp was just a huge pond; It was about 1 meter deep but looks like a swamp because of the size of land it has covered. No wild animals and no poisonous insects. It was indeed smooth sailing for Mark. This story has identified three types of dreamers in this world; those who easily gives up, those who are goal getters but follows a traditional approach and is afraid of taking risks, and those who are willing to take the shortcut and face the risks. Yes, the way around the swamp would also get you to the treasure, however, with the competition that we have in this world, before you get the promotion you want, someone else must have taken it already because of the time you wasted by not choosing the better option. Have yourself ready and take the risks. You are for sure is to succeed in life.

Professionalism

In the professional work environment, avoid dramas, and just do your job. Professionalism to the highest level will make life easier for you. Lessen the friendship and just establish a colleague-type of relationship with everyone. This would allow you to focus on why you are there in the first place; to conquer the hierarchical ladder of success.

Self-Love

If you have you heard yourself saying any of these; "I love my girlfriend/boyfriend more than I love myself", "I rather die than to see my family suffer", "I'd rather choose to suffer for the benefit of others", and others alike, you are a disappointment. Many will disagree to me on this, but how will you love others, if you can't love yourself. Everything starts from you, especially the recognition and the value you deserve. Shedding light to the life of others will not brighten yours, in fact, it will lessen it. I am not telling you to be greedy; you just have to understand that in getting to your goal faster, it is important that you focus first on yourself that extending hands to others who have their own goals in life.

There may be no elevator to success and that everyone has to take the stairs, but if you are going to cover two steps at a time, you will reach the top first
Mark Gabriel Wagan Aguilar

CHAPTER 3

GETTING TO YOUR
GOAL

Everybody may not agree with you, but that does not make them right and makes you wrong. Let your success speaks for you
Prof. Mark Gabriel Wagan Aguilar

The risk of believing in the wrong path

Do you think it is really the years of experience? Do you really think it is the reputation of your previous employer? Do you think that it is your loyalty to the company that will take you to the promotion you ever wanted? We all know that there are several stories where people who have been with the company for decades but end up becoming subordinates of people who just came in. Do you want to know their secret? They have chosen the better way, unlike you who have believed in a mistake.

Have you seen a group of people taking the stairs to get to the 2nd floor? Assuming that they have stood on the first step and started climbing at the same time; do they all arrive at the top simultaneously, as in at the same time? Someone stepped first on the last step, right? There may be no physical shortcut to your goal and everyone has to go through the same road, but remember, you don't have to do the same way others are doing it, you can always do things differently. When you take the stairs, you may choose to climb the stairs one step at a time, while you may also choose to cover two steps every move. And you may choose to have a 1-2 seconds interval between your steps, while you may also choose to move your feet faster. Keep in mind, everyone has gone through the same road, but it does not mean that they will all reach the other end of it within the same timeframe. Keep in mind that it is how you did it, and not what you did. Change your beliefs, change your ways, and get yourself to the top.

Wrong believing puts people in a prison. Right believing is a light that illuminates the path to freedom out of this prison

Joseph Prince

Seven Ingredients that will pave your way to success

Build Connection

Build a network! A person who doesn't have a circle of friends in the professional work environment is less likely to succeed in life. However, when building your network, you must be selective; limit yourself to befriending only those to whom you could benefit from and those who have already proven something in life. Focus only on people who are better than you, thus, forget those who have been a baggage to you, as Confucius once said *"never contract friendship with a man that is not better than thyself"*. Befriends those on the higher levels of the ladder, they will serve as your access to better opportunities.

Join social media groups, create a professional online account, and apply for membership in various professional associations. Building a network should be continuous; the wider connection you have, the faster you'd be able to get to the top.

Learn everyday

Learning is a never ending process; it should not stop after college. Education is the best investment as it cannot be stolen from you. People think that education is luxury, but what most of us don't know is there are a lot of affordable courses that are accessible by anyone by just having the will to learn. Top Universities from all parts of the globe have been offering "Massive open online courses", which some are totally from registration to exams to claiming your certificate of completion. You have heard it right, Online Certificate Courses from Harvard, MIT, and Oxford University for a zero fee. These courses may not be degrees, but these are recognized by companies all over the world. These indeed will make your curriculum vitae more attractive, establish you credibility, and will make you more employable and promotable. Scholarly works will also give you more advantages over others; you should not just rely on what other people have written, have your own discoveries, conduct a research, and then publish it. Book authorship is also another key; writing a book will make you stand out from the rest. Continue learning, never stop, die learning, and let others learn from you as well.

Change your way, not your Goal

Many of us tend to think that changing our goal is the best to achieve something in life. This is another wrong decision that we have been making through the years. What we don't realize is by changing the goal, the more you deny yourself access to what you really want to achieve. Remember, there is no impossible goal; the only reason why it is taking you too long to get there is because you are doing it wrong. Process is important, without doing things right and by not choosing the better way; success will really be hesitant to show itself to you. Never stop trying you until get there. Goals will always be unreachable for us, until we finally reach it.

Learn to sacrifice

Prioritization! Ask yourself, what is your priority in life? Is it reaching your dreams or something else? You should know how to weight things in life, and yes, time will come that you have drop some things in order to keep on moving towards your goal. There are time when you have to choose between getting to your goal or accomplishing something else that is also important to you, but this is life, you simply can't have everything. Do you want that promotion even if your friend wants it so bad; it may cost you your friendship? Do you want that opportunity overseas even if you won't be able be with your family for several years? Do you want that managerial position offered by a competing establishment despite the relationship you have with your boss for working with them for several years? Ask yourself, how much do you want that goal? Are you willing to let go something important to you just for it? That is how it works; you really have to make yourself ready to sacrifice.

Get inspired by others

In life, you need to have a role model. Having someone who you see as an inspiration because of what he/she has accomplished in life, will motivate you to work harder and be better. Learning about the stories of great men creates a mindset that there is nothing impossible. But aside from getting inspired by their stories, I professionally suggest you to criticize their ways, and come up with your own that you see as more effective and efficient. The main purpose of acquiring that drive from others is not to replicate what they have done to reach their goals, but to conceptualize improved ways so that you can reach greater heights.

Choose the right employer

Does your company recognize your contributions as an employee? Does your workplace have an open work environment? Does your employer opens up or at least permit personal and professional development opportunities to you? Does your employer bases the credibility and promotability of an employee on performance and capability than tenure of service? Are you able to establish a quality professional relationship with your immediate superior? At least one no answer to these questions is a sign that you should resign from your job immediately. The more you stay there, the more you deny yourself a clearer access to your goals in life. An employer that does not give you recognitions despite your hard work is insensitive, thus, sees you as robot with a responsibility to do your job. An employer who does not create an open work environment for its employees will never see you as part of the success of the company.

While a company that does not expose its employees to professional development opportunities is self-centered; focusing only on the money coming in and not seeing their employees succeed. And an employer that believes tenure of service is more important than an employee's capability is nothing but a company that is bound to fail.

When choosing an employer, make sure that your beliefs correspond to what culture does the company has. You attitude and the way you see things should blend well to the mission and vision of the company, and as well as to the management approach being practiced by the top management. It is important that the company where you will start your journey towards your goal have the ability to push you to become a better version of yourself and will motivate you to keep going despite challenges. Ask yourself, are you motivated by monetary rewards and benefits? Are you motivated by the feeling of having a significant role in the organization? Does getting the position and the type of work you really want is enough for you? Or does recognition and promotion is what keeps you going? Whatever serves a motivation to you, you should see it in your employer, or else you will just be exposed to an environment that won't get you any nearer to your goal.

Choose the company that believes in you, trusts your capabilities, and empowers your knowledge and skills.

Enjoy the little things

Pressuring and pushing yourself to the limit to achieve your goals, may be sometimes tiring. No matter how committed and determined you are, your mind and body needs time to rejuvenate after a long tiring journey. To keep yourself going and excited, find time to rest and celebrate the little things that you have already done. You need this to remind yourself that there is something happening, that your hard work is really paying off, and that you are getting nearer and nearer to your goal. Reward yourself for a job well done. Even work towards your goal needs a day off. On the way to your journey, you still need to stop by a gas station and get refueled.

As you go on to your journey, it is also important that you keep a record of what you are doing and have accomplished. It is just right to know where exactly you are already. Getting lost in the midst of reaching our goals in life is a common dilemma, thus, you should keep track of your progress. Setting a timeframe would also do good, but might decrease your drive especially if you see that you have not accomplished that much within a period of time. Instead of looking at it that way, let your shortcomings be your motivation to work harder and fight tougher. Success is for the strong, Failure is for the weak. Be strong and reach your goals quick.

> ***Try to discover the road to success and you'll seek but never find, but blaze your own path and the road to success will trail right behind***
>
> ***Robert Brault***

The key to success is not found by anybody, it is only you who knows what is best for you, but with proper guidance from people who have been there and done that, you will get there faster and easier.

CHAPTER IV

TELLING YOUR SUCCESS STORY AND INSPIRING OTHERS

Conquering the hierarchical ladder is an achievement, but producing people better than you is a legacy
Prof. Mark Gabriel Wagan Aguilar

Sharing your story

Inform everybody the story of your success, and keep on maintaining that fire in you by giving a hand to others. Sharing your story is not about bragging or being proud; sharing what you have been through and how you have overcome it, is about establishing hope in others hearts and the recognition you may receive from them, which will motivate you to keep on reaching greater heights. Your progress should never stop, thus, your commitment, hard work, focus, risk-taking attitude, self-love, positivity, competitive attitude, humility, professionalism, and sense of urgency shall remain as part of your personality. Inspiring others and securing that success are going to be your next goals.

Sharing your story however, can be difficult. There are several ways on how can tell it to everybody; you may write a book, render speeches at events, train your employees, or personally speak to one person to another.

Whatever way you choose, make sure that they have received what you meant; this is the only sign that you are telling a good story and is bound to leaving a legacy.

Inspiring others is not just to motivate them, but also to remind yourself of all the lessons you have learned in life. This will also inspire you and make you realize how strong and smart you are. Self - Appreciation has a huge contribution to your holistic development, which you need to properly deal with life and society.

When you stand and share your story in an empowering way, your story will heal you and your story will somebody else

Iyanla Vanzant

Inspire others and teach them how to fish

Inspire others with your story only after you have succeeded, and not light a lamp for them while you are still trying to light yours! Learn to love yourself first, before loving someone else. Lighting up the path of someone else won't brighten up yours. Once you have reached the top of the ladder, it is not time to look down and become the access of others. You may give them a hand, but never pull them up! Just hold them so that if they make mistakes, they won't fall back to the first step. You as an inspiration is going to be reason why they won't make mistakes anymore, just like how you have used your connections, your role model, and the stories of great men. But they will still be the one to push themselves towards their goals, just like what you did when you were paving the road to your own success.

Inspire others and help them to get out of the wall surrounding them, limiting their movements, and stopping them from getting to their goals. Teach them how to fish; teach them how to move on their own and get them to understand the value of the six ingredients to reaching a goal in life.

Be a mentor; listen to them, if you are a manager, get to know your people. Ask them what they really want in life and listen carefully to how they plan to achieve it. From this stage, you would be able to know how you will be able to help them. A good mentor also makes sure that his students really know what they are doing and are thinking to do; ask the people around you why they have chosen such goal, how important is this them, and how has it been seen they started working on it. Shed them light and positivity, especially those who have a negative attitude towards their dreams. Encourage them and show them the light behind the darkness that they see. As their mentor, never leave them, and continue guide them throughout the way. Understand that by standing beside them, you would be able to bring yourself to their success, and achieve what most success stories don't have, successfully produce people better than you.

Motivating others leads to success whereas inspiring others leads to greatness

Ken Poirot

BONUS CHAPTERS

MANAGING BUSINESS SUCCESSFULLY

What makes a Successful Business Manager?

Success in the field of Business starts with your instinct; only you can say if business is really your calling or not. You must have an overwhelming desire to have your own business. Time is so precious to be wasted on something you really don't want to do, which will not lead you to satisfaction and happiness. A business that is bound to succeed will surely fail if this industry is not really for you. Alongside with your desire to put up a business, having enough capital and intelligence is needed. To become a successful business manager, you should have the knowledge towards the kind of business that you want to put before turning it to reality. You may have a lot of money, but if you don't know how the industry works, you are more likely to be spending your money for nothing.

It is also highly important that the business you are planning to put up is where you are passionate about and is what you do best; never ever enter a business from the ideas of others. Your family and friends may give you advices based on trends and your personality, but make sure that it is from where the final decision came from.

Next, make sure that you have the enough funds to support your attempt. The money that you will need is not just for your products, equipment to be used to provide services, and location. You have to make sure that you have funds for your marketing and promotion that will give the public information about your products and services, for insurance to make sure that if anything goes wrong you will be able to recover, and other essential elements of business such as manpower, partnership, and legal processes.

Not getting many persons to work for you during the first months to a year of your business is recommended to minimize the capital needed, thus, having yourself as part of the ground operations will be a huge help.

One you have estimated the capital you need and have it ready, it is time to choose which location your business has to be.

Choosing a location is one of the toughest stages in putting up your business. To determine your target market, know your resources and the things needed for your business, determine accessibility, and assess the volume of traffic, are just few of the actions that you have to take in order to come up with the ideal location for your business. It may be a physical store or an online one.

The Do's and Don'ts in Managing a Business

Do's

- **Save more and Spend less**

  Businesses' primary objective is to make money and to continuously do that is evidence that a business is successful. In business, a businessman can only say that he is earning money from his business if he was able to earn more than his capital and is able to earn more than the money he releases for marketing, promotions, product development, among others, thus, it is advisable for businessmen to make sure that they are spending less than what they are actually earning from the business. I know that it can get quite overwhelming after getting that first revenue report but you have to save to make sure that your business will still be on track even after problems arose. If you are just in the first year of doing business, it is highly recommended that you just spend the money earned from your business to resources needed by the business; no personal purchases yet until the next year of success.

- **Work in an establishment or company that has the same line of services and products as the business you plan to put up.**

   Learn from the experts! Learning how to do business is really tough especially if you don't have any background on it. To benchmark is the best way through this challenge, but nothing would be better if you yourself are taught by companies who have been big the business industry. By learning from them, you'd be able to know everything including the ups and downs of business management.

- **Take advantage of free distribution channels**

  There are several ways on how we can market, promote, and deliver our products and services for free. What makes it more interesting is that some of these platforms generate the highest traffic. The best example for this is facebook. In the Philippines, an average of 10 hours a day is spent by Filipinos in the internet mostly on facebook; this is way higher than the country's average time of watching television that has recorded only 4.9 hours per week.

- **Consider starting from small**

  Slowly but surely as they say, this is actually effective for most entrepreneurs. Though some may disagree, this is the best way to successfully penetrate in the market if you are a neophyte.

- **Know your competitors**

  In a lot of competitions, coaches usually advise their players to focus on their game and not to their competitor'. However, in business, it is the other way around; in fact a SWOT analysis should be a part of your business plan where you should conduct a research about your competitors in order to know the best practices that you have to apply in your business to get ahead of them. There are 3 reasons why you need to know your competitors well; 1. To be able to develop products and services better than what they offer, 2. To be able compete within their market share and get a chance to attract more customers, 3. To know your weaknesses and the reason why they are on top and you are not.

- **Consider Low-Cost manufacturing for your products**

  Low-Cost Manufacture is going to help you lot if you are just starting to establish a name in the business industry; it will enable you to spend a lot on producing your products and services, thus, minimize your expenses. Low-Cost does not always mean cheap or under the quality standard, you can still guarantee quality by following ethics in product development.

- **Constantly conduct intensive market researches**

  If there is one thing that is a challenge to businesses, it is the changing buying behavior and preference of the market. Trends changes overnight and it is a big loss to the business if you won't be able to determine those changes. Knowing your market very well will enable you to offer the products and services that they really need and want. This will also enable you to identify the right market segment for you and find out how you can attract them to buy from you and keep on coming back.

- **Talk to people for advice**
Learn continuously. Listen to people. If you are big company and you have people working for you, it is better if you will establish an open work environment. An open work environment will empower your employees and will motivate them to make suggestion for the betterment of the business. Try to have consultants as well, they might see something wrong with processes and policies that you implement, which you have not seen. Communication is good. Listen so that you could learn more.

- **Benchmark**

  Benchmarking is best if you are starting a business, if you are thinking of new marketing plan, and if you are to develop a product. Take a look at businesses that have made a name already, get inspired by their strategies and policies; from there, you would be able to adapt it or conceptualize a better one.

- **Encourage customers' feedbacks**

  This is very important. Aside from knowing what your customers' experiences are, feedbacks is way of saying to the market that you listen to them and you care of what they think. However, getting costumers' feedback is not enough; make sure that you will also improve your products and services guided by it. Action is important, but of course it is after knowing what are needed to be done.

Don'ts

- Leave your jobs before achieving a stable business operations
- Force yourself to love a line of business you dislike
- Put all the assets you have on the business
- Rush yourself to entering the business industry
- Start from business that requires too much capital and acquires many expenses
- Compromise quality over quantity
- Avoid learning the negative side of business
- Establish a very confidence
- Start without a contingency plan
- Replicate the products of your competitors

MANAGING YOUR PEOPLE EFFECTIVELY

The Art of People Management

What many don't recognize is the importance of their employees towards the continuous success of their business. Your people aside from your customers are the backbone of the business, they have the power to make or break everything that you have worked for over the years. In service-oriented establishments, it is the employees who provide the services to customers, thus, they are the primary reason of satisfaction as well as disappointment, while in a product-oriented company like those in the manufacturing line of business, it is the employees who make the production possible, thus, they are the primary reason why you continuously hit that production target every day that gives a competitive advantages to your business over your competitors. As a matter of fact, the employees based on what they do and it impact your business can be considered as your business partners, and it is just right to recognize them as if they are. Recognize your employees and they will recognize you. Disregarding their position; they act as an essential part of the operations and is one of the reason why your business is still sharing a part of the market. Keep in mind also that a high people attrition rate is bad for business; this will expose you to the risk of losing experienced employees and getting neophytes as replacement. Continue doing business as you maintain your manpower, and you are more likely to reach the top.

The Do's and Don'ts of Human Resource Management

Do's

- **Carefully select your people**

  It is very important that you get only the right people to work for you, when hiring, consider professional experiences, educational background, and communication skills. Most employers nowadays will say that attitude should be evaluated during the hiring stage, however, there a very limited ways to determine the real attitude of a person. Get as many applicants as you can before starting the screening process; the risks of getting wrong people to do the job for you is very high.

- **Thoroughly check the background of hopefuls**

  During an interview, most applicants will do their best to establish a good image to you; however, there is a chance that they are just playing you so they could get the job. One way to verify their resume and their personality is to conduct a thorough background check. Conducting a background check will cost you time and effort, reason why most employers nowadays just rely to phone calls and e-mail. This is problem; we have been doing it wrong. Our applicants can always ask give you a random number and a self-made email address, besides, how you can tell if you are really talking to his/her previous supervisor or just his friend reading a script. It is better if you will visit his/her previous company and ask the supervisor itself; this is better than to risk the success of your business.

- **Provide a clear job description and a well presented Employees' Manual**

  Coming up with a policy will do nothing if your employees do not have a clear information and access on it. A manual that will detailed present rules and regulations will do the job. Another problem encountered by employers is their employees' lack of awareness towards their jobs; to avoid this, make sure that prior signing the contract, they are already know what they getting themselves into.

- **Provide a competitive employee benefits package for loyalty and performance**

  If you have found good people to work for you, the next thing you have to do is make them stay. Based on several researches, employees stay for the following reasons; 1. They are being paid right, 2. They are being heard,

3. They are happy, and 4. They feel needed. Competition is also a challenge when trying to keep your people with you; your best employees might get attracted to offers of other companies, and in worst cases, it is the company who will try corrupt employees of others.

- **Establish a partnership with at least one labor lawyer to avoid expensive claims and penalties**
Be smart and make sure that your decisions won't lead you to losses. Hiring a lawyer who will be in touch with you and available whenever needed is highly recommended. This will also help in dealing with legal documents, making sure that your products and services abide the law, and avoid problems with your people.

- **Assess potential employees by educational background, skills, and personality**

  Your employees should be a complete package, however, during the recruitment process, it very difficult to know the real personality of a person. When considering someone for a job, it is better to rely on what his/her Curriculum Vitae says than how he acts in front of you and what he says during an interview. The credentials of an applicant is the proof of his credibility and reliability, unless he/she is lying but that is the reason why you still need thorough background check. Skills comes in second since you will be seeing it once the applicant is already working with the company, and third is personality which you will be able to observe as time passes by.

- **Open up professional development opportunities for your employees**

  One of the motivations why people will choose to stay with a company is professional development. They would appreciate if you will open up opportunities for them to improve and become better persons and develop their skills in the field that they have chosen. Sponsor seminars for them, and organize trainings with focus on the skills where they need to improve. This will not just make them feel that you care for them but will also ensure your company quality products and services since it is your employees who act as providers.

- **Observe strict implementation of the 5S system**

  5S's is derive from five Japanese terms starting with letter "S" used a guide to create a more organized and productive workplace. The first S is Seiri that means to separate needed things and instructions from unneeded materials. Unneeded ones are advised to be thrown away. The second S is Seiton, which means to neatly arrange and identify things for ease of use. The third S is Seiso, which aims to create a clean surrounding. The fourth is called Seiketsu that means to conduct seiri, seiton, and seiso daily to maintain a workplace in good condition. And the last S is Shitsuke that aims to form the habit of always following the first 4 S's.

- **Maintain an open work environment**
An open work environment means giving your people freedom to express and have say for the betterment of the company. By doing this, you would be able to make your employees feel that they are valued and an important part of whatever success the company will

achieve. This can be done through freedom wall, a suggestion box, and by just simply giving them access to your office. There is a lot of ways to create an open work environment, but whatever ways you will be implementing within your organization, it is important that it gives equal chances for everybody disregarding their positions.

Don'ts

- Delay in terminating poor-performing employees
- Overlook an employee's knowledge, skills, and passion
- Give employees tasks that are not stated in their job description without their consent
- Overlook the reward system for your employees
- Have a personal relationship with your employees

Best Practices in People Management

The following practices are based on my perspective as a leader as the results of my experiences from being a student leader during my college years to being the School Director of an International College today.

- MGWA

Put the right people in the right places

To maximize the productivity of your subordinates and the organization, put your people in the positions where their personality and ability fit well. Initially, put them in the positions which they applied for after, but as they spend time working with the organization, monitor their performance, study them, and evaluate their knowledge and skills. This will give you a clear vision whether they are fit in the positions that they have chosen. People are sometimes confused between what they like to do and where they will really perform best. As a leader, you need to guide your people and this includes putting them in positions where they are more likely to be productive, not just for them, but for the success of your company.

Implement a general rule but apply different approaches to different personalities.

Establish a culture that will be followed by your people, but have a different approach when dealing to one person to another. If you are managing a Higher Education Institution for example, establish a formal and professional culture but when talking to your people, apply various communication approaches depending on one's personality. Understand that your employees came from different walks of life, they have different beliefs, and they were raised by their parents in different ways. There are members of your team who are sensitive to a high tone of voice, while there are some who prefers an authoritarian approach. To fully get your people moving the way you want them to move, make sure that you know them and you are able to apply the proper approach when dealing with them.

Establish a strict, perfectionist, and professional image

Generally show a Boss-Type leadership approach. The purpose of this is to hold your organization intact and avoiding any mess. Having your people follow one path makes sure that the organization is bound to where it should go. No Dramas, Just Work. However, I professionally advise you to be careful as you enforce this kind of leadership style; make sure that the people see the progress of what you are all doing, which will give them a clear understanding on why you are like that. But if they would feel that despite the cage-like work environment nothing is happening, they would probably talk behind your back and worst leave you with problems. This approach is good to ensure the success of the company but is risky when it comes to retention of employees.

Hold regularly meetings

If there is one thing that a leader should never forget is to hold meetings regularly. At least twice a month is needed depending on the size of your organization; the bigger the more meetings you should organize with your team. Through meetings, you should be able to give your team about progress and challenges your organization is experiencing. Regularly meeting your people in one room also gives the impression of an open work environment since they are given an opportunity to talk to you and communicate with other departments. This will also give you an opportunity to know about updates of their tasks and projects, and to check how they are all doing. I encourage you to find time to check on your people; there is no harm in asking your people how was their experience with a project, how is life in general, and if they have problem, at least give advises and tap them at the back. Meet your employees and build a stronger organization where everybody knows each other, thus, would allow a healthier professional relationship.

Maintain a high visibility

If you spend all your duty hours inside your office, resign now and never come back. If you are managing a big organization; a school, hotel, restaurant, business firms, and any establishment that has several departments; you should spend 10-20% of your time everyday outside your office. You should visit offices, chat with people going in and out your company, and sit in a public area; whatever you do, make sure that in a day, your people get to see you. This will give them an impression that you are aware of what is happening on the ground and that you are there watching over them. A good leader knows what is really happening in the operation by personally seeing it, and not just what the interior of his office looks like. Get out there and show them that you are really involved in the operations.

Walk the Talk

Lead them by example. Implement rules and regulations that also include you. Whatever you say, make sure that it will not backfire on you by embodying it. Learn the culture and the standard operation procedures of the company like what you instructed your people to do. You will continuously fail to make your people follow you, if you can't present yourself as an example.

Show them how to do it

Are you not satisfied on how the janitor swept the floor? Get the mop and show him how to do it; sweep the floor while he is watching. Keep in mind that your employees are people, they make mistakes, and so do you. A leader leads the way and do not just point the direction where to go, but walks with his people towards the goal. You are not just teaching them, you are also minimizing the risk of committing mistakes, thus, would save your organization possible losses. Teaching them the right way to do things would also develop them until they become independent. Be a part of your people's success, and they will truly love their jobs; this will enable you to have happy, loyal, and competent employees.

Performance is more important than Attitude

Most if not all successful leaders around the world would disagree to this, but if you will weight things out, you will find out that the success of any business really does depends on the performance of your employees in the jobs assigned to them. Attitude is what binds people within an organization, but performance is what keeps the organization alive and kicking. Attitude is easy to modify using the right approach, but performance to improve takes a lot of time and efforts. This is the reason why opening up professional development opportunities to your people is highly recommended. Being kind and sensitive will never compensate intelligence and skills, at least in the professional work environment.

Talk to your people if there is a problem

Avoid learning about conflicts involving someone within your organization from somebody else. Open yourself to your people regarding work-relevant problems and challenges they encounter. If necessary and possible, I encourage you to sometimes open your door or at least use a glass door to give an impression that you are open for a talk with them. By doing so, you save yourself and your organization from hearsays and issues left unsolved prior to getting to your knowledge. As a leader, you should be able know the problems immediately to avoid getting worse.

About the Author

Born and raised in the Philippines, Professor Mark Gabriel Wagan Aguilar, "Gab" to his friends and colleagues started learning about life, the environment at a very young age with the guidance of his grandfather, Dr. Ricardo Apolinario Wagan who has been his motivation to greatness. Dr. Wagan who is President of a University, Chairman of an Association of University Presidents, and a Reservist of the Philippine Army has exposed Gab to responsibilities that will teach him the reality of life. At first, this lifestyle has established a negative perspective to Gab's mind; he hated all the rules and the things he has to do every day just to satisfy his grandfather, but as time passes by, he have realized that all his grandfather wants is to instill discipline in him and train him to what he will be facing in the professional work environment.

The two used to spend the last hour of the day together talking about life, leadership, and success, which has been his ticket to achieve all of his goals in life, create a mindset that success can be achieved without spending too much time, and that one should always keep on looking for opportunities and shall never get satisfied.

As a student, Gab was not ordinary. He is the President of the highest governing student body of the University, which has exposed him to a lot of challenges and opportunities, thus, made him strong and independent. He graduated at the age of 20 from Laguna State Polytechnic University with a Bachelor's Degree in Tourism, not long enough was able to land a job in an International Hotel and Serviced Residences in Makati City as a Concierge Executive cum Bell Hop. Since what he really want is to act as a mentor to people, and he enjoys being listened to; he turned his attention to the academe. He left the Tourism Industry and started to teach few classes in a local University. Hungry for continuous professional development, he attended seminars and classes that gave him access not just to education but to networking opportunities. In one of his classes, he met an owner of a travel agency who later became his boss as a Travel Consultant; he pursued his career in the academe simultaneously with his job in the travel agency to maximize the time in obtaining relevant knowledge and experience that would boost his credibility as a professional.

He never stopped widening his network; he pursued courses in the Philippines and abroad, and devoted time and effort to research and other scholarly works. From 2017 to 2019, he was able to finish a number of Certificate courses in Tourism, Educational Management, Environmental Sustainability, and Business, and in less than a year, he was able to publish a number of researches in International Newsletters and Journals.

After spending 2 years in the Tourism Industry and 3 years as an Educator, he was able to sustain his success by proving his capability. Currently, he is the School Director of an International College in Metro Manila that offers Senior High School

Courses and Baccalaureate Programs in Business and Real Estate Management. As the School Director, he holds the highest position in the campus, and is responsible in the overall operations of the Institution.

For Prof. Aguilar, people management and decision making skills are the most important skills a leader needs to have. It is actually where he focused on as he pursues his journey towards success. The School Director aside from the degree and certificate courses he has pursued is a Certified Tourism and Hospitality Professional, Certified Negotiation Associate, and Certified in Content Marketing; all awarded by International Certification Giving Bodies based in the United States of America and United Kingdom.

With his achievements, no doubt that Prof. Aguilar is one of the few who were able to conquer the hierarchical ladder of success in a very fast way.

The Author

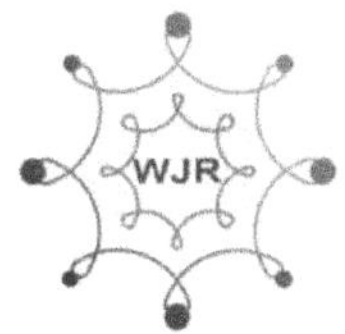

Editorial Board Member
Worldwide Journal of Research

Editorial Board Member
J. of Tourism & Sports Mgmt.

Editorial Board Member
Int'l J. of Research Publications

Prof. Aguilar is also a member of the following International Organizations:

Int'l Association for Community Devt.

International Social Marketing Association

Social Sci. & Humanities Research Assoc.

Teaching & Education Research Association

Healthcare & Biological Sciences
Research Association

International Sustainable Development
Research Society

International Tourism Association of
Professionals

World Economics Association

International Management Research and Technology Consortium

Prof. Aguilar has authored the following researches:

TOURISM AND HOSPITALITY MANAGEMENT DEGREES AS PERCEIVED BY THE INDUSTRY: A NECESSITY OR JUST A WORTHLESS OPTION
International Research Journal of Social Sciences
ISSN: 2319 - 3565
Date Received: May 2, 2020 (on review process)

ATTITUDE VERSUS PRACTICES OF THE LOCAL COMMUNITY OF LOS BAÑOS, LAGUNA, PHILIPPINES TOWARD ECOTOURISM
International Research Journal of Environmental Sciences
ISSN: 2319 - 1414
Date Received: April 27, 2020 (on review process)

THE TOURISM BUSINESS INDUSTRY OF THE MUNICIPALITY OF TANAY, RIZAL, PHILIPPINES: AN ASSESSMENT ON HUMAN RESOURCE AND A PROVINCE-WIDE MARKET RESEARCH
Journal of Tourism Management Research
ISSN: 2313-4178
Date Accepted: April 27, 2020 (on publication process)

PROVINCIAL PERSPECTIVE TOWARDS TOURISM INDUSTRY PRODUCTS IN CALAMBA CITY, LAGUNA, PHILIPPINES: A BASIS FOR BUSINESS PLANNING AND DEVELOPMENT
Journal of Tourism and Sports Management
Volume 1, Issue 2, pp. 112-133
Date Published: May 11, 2020

INDUSTRIAL REVOLUTION AND THE
MARKET'S PERSPECTIVE
TOWARDS THE BUSINESS INDUSTRY: A
MACRO ANALYSIS
International Journal of Trends in Scientific
Research and Development
Volume 4, Issue 3, pp. 720-724
Date Published: April 15, 2020

SOCIAL MEDIA, FILIPINOS, AND KEY
NATIONAL ISSUES IN THE PHILIPPINES: A
MACRO ANALYSIS
Int'l J. of Research and Innovation in Social Science
Volume 4, Issue 4, pp. 1-3
Date Published: April 15, 2020

STRENGTHENING SOCIETIES AND FAMILIES
THROUGH STRICT LIFE PLANNING AND
FAMILY-BUILDING POLICY: A BASIS FOR
NATIONAL POLICY CREATION AND
AMENDMENTS
International Journal of Research Publications
Volume 50, Issue 1, pp. 67-78
Date Published: April 10, 2020

SEX TOURISM IN THE PHILIPPINES: A BASIS
FOR PLANNING, AND POLICY MAKING AND
AMENDMENTS
Journal of Tourism and Hospitality
Volume 8, Issue 5, pp. 12-18
Date Published: October 24, 2019

INCLUSIVE TOURISM AND THE
MUNICIPALITY OF LOBO, BATANGAS,
PHILIPPINES: A BASIS FOR PLANNING AND
DEVELOPMENT
IACD Membership Blog, Article No. 2
International Association for Community
Development
Scotland, United Kingdom
Date Published: September 5, 2019

The most powerful statements toward success in the Author's Perspective

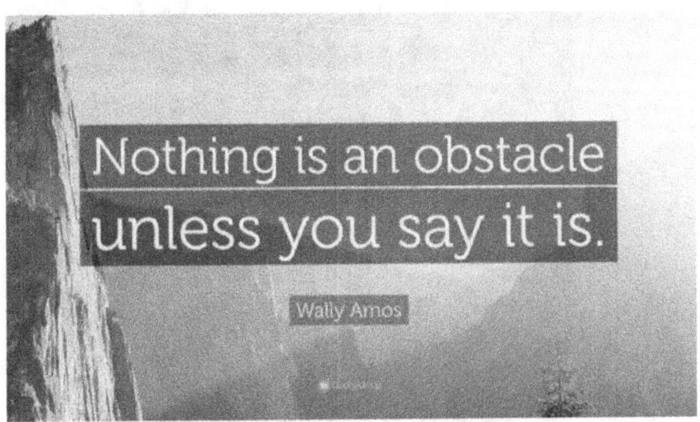

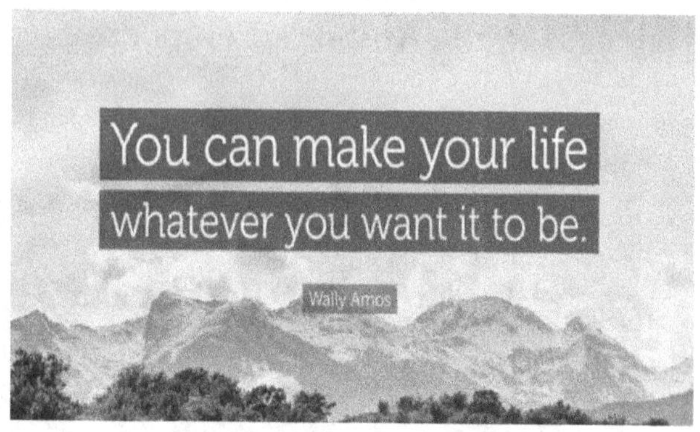
You can make your life
whatever you want it to be.
Wally Amos

WHEN NOTHING BUT
THE BEST IS
EXPECTED, NOTHING
BUT THE BEST IS
DELIVERED
#MOTIVATIONALMONDAYS

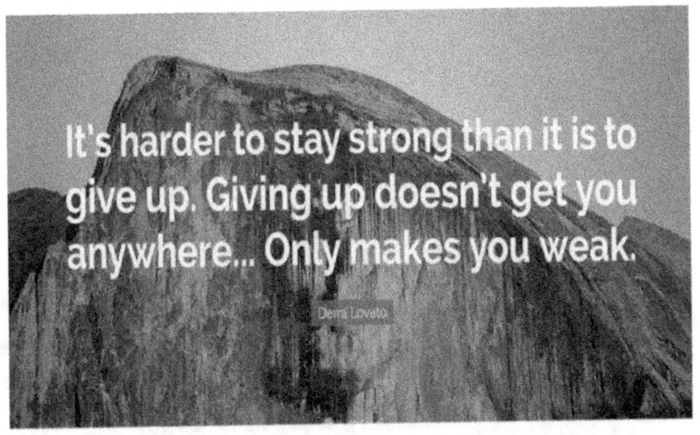
It's harder to stay strong than it is to give up. Giving up doesn't get you anywhere... Only makes you weak.
Demi Lovato

Unity is strength...
when there
is teamwork
and collaboration,
wonderful
things can be
achieved.
Mattie Stepanek

OBSTACLES ARE PUT IN YOUR WAY TO HELP YOU DETERMINE IF WHAT YOU WANT IS REALLY WORTH FIGHTING FOR.

PictureQuotes.com

My dreams are worthless, my plans are dust, my goals are impossible. All are of no value unless they are followed by action.

Og Mandino

NOTES

This is a space where you could write an outline of what you have picked up from this book. This will help you in reminding yourself about what your goals are and how should you run towards it